RUFUS
THE
DOOFUS

NED DELANEY

Houghton Mifflin Company Boston 1978

Library of Congress Cataloging in Publication Data

Delaney, Ned.
 Rufus the Doofus.

 SUMMARY: Rufus is ignored by his classmates until
he becomes the holy terror of the class, but a moment of
friendship restores him to his own true amiable self.
 [1. Friendship—Fiction. 2. School stories]
I. Title.
PZ7.D3732Ru   [E]   78-60493
ISBN 0-395-27153-3

Rufus sat by himself in the back of the class.

3

No one ever paid any attention to Rufus.
Miss Wirble, the teacher, never called on him
when he raised his hand. None of Rufus' classmates
ever copied his answers during a test.

His only friends were the fish in the fishbowl.

Rufus liked the fish and he thought they liked him, too.

On the playground, Rufus was never picked for a team and was always left out of the games. So he searched for food to feed to the fish. He captured caterpillars. He collected crumbs from Tilly's saltines. He even caught the flies buzzing over Mortimer, who never took a bath.

No one ever noticed Rufus.

One day at lunch, Rufus filled his bowl with worm chowder.
He took a step and tripped. The chowder sailed into
the air and, KERPLAT! landed all over Zelda.
"UHHG," said Zelda.

Everyone laughed.

"Great prank, Rufus," said Leroy.

"They noticed me!" thought Rufus.

He gave Zelda a pinch.

"And I thought Rufus was a square," said Ruby.

"GRRR," said Rufus.

Early next morning, Rufus sprinkled pepper on the geology
books. He drew a horrible picture on the blackboard. The
class sneezed when they sat down. Miss Wirble nearly
fainted when she saw the blackboard.

"Who could have done such a thing?" Miss Wirble asked.

"RRRR," said Rufus.

During recess, Rufus was the terror of the playground.
He squirted glue on the slide.
He spread peanut butter on the swings.

"It was Rufus," someone said.
"ARRR," said Rufus.

At lunch, Rufus flipped mashed potatoes with his fork. He gurgled his milk. He put worms into the spaghetti and soap between the sandwiches.

"What a doofus!" the class cried.
"RRRR," said Rufus.

Rufus jammed ants down Oscar's trousers.
He slipped spiders down Tilly's back.
"YEOWCH," said Oscar.
"YUCK," said Tilly.
"ARRR," said Rufus.

When Miss Wirble reached into her desk drawer for an eraser,
she pulled out a pair of Mortimer's smelly gym socks.
"Rufus!" said Miss Wirble. "Stop acting like a wild animal
and go sit in the corner."
"GRRR," said Rufus.

Rufus went and sat in the corner.

Then the door of the room opened and there stood the
prettiest creature Rufus had ever seen.

"Class," said Miss Wirble, "meet Maybelline Mergatroid,
our new pupil. Now I have to go next door to correct tests.
There will be no biting or clawing while I'm away."

"Maybelline looks like a swell wrestler," said Ruby.

"I bet Maybelline is a terrific Ping-Pong player,"
said Leroy.

"Maybelline will be marvelous on our horseshoe team,"
said Zelda.

Rufus just thought Maybelline would make a good friend.

The class did everything they could think of to
impress Maybelline.

"Watch me flex my muscles," said Mortimer.

"How silly," said Maybelline.

Rufus wished there was something special he could do.

"Hey, Maybelline," said Mortimer, "watch me do my
snazzy double somersault!"
"What a showoff," thought Rufus. "I'll fix him."
No one saw Rufus tie Mortimer's tail to the table.

Mortimer tried his somersault.

The table crashed to the floor. The fishbowl flew into the air and landed on Mortimer's head. The fish flopped helplessly on the floor.

"Someone save the fish!" yelled Maybelline.

"My fish!" cried Rufus.

He quickly scooped the fish off the floor and slipped them into the flower vase on Miss Wirble's desk.

"Rufus saved the fish!" said Maybelline.

Mortimer began to turn blue.

"He can't breathe!" the class cried. "Save Mortimer!"

No one could get the fishbowl off Mortimer's head.
"It's my fault," said Rufus. "Let me try."

"I'll hold the fishbowl and everyone pull Mortimer's tail,"
cried Rufus.
They tugged and tugged. Mortimer turned bluer and bluer.
"Yank!" said Rufus.
POP! The fishbowl flew off Mortimer's head.

Mortimer caught his breath.

"Boy, Rufus," said Mortimer, "you're the pits!"

"Someone who cares for fish could never be the pits,"
said Maybelline.

"Ahh, who cares about crummy fish?" said Mortimer.

"I care about fish," said Rufus.

"And I care about fish," said Maybelline.

"And we all care about Rufus, too," everyone said.

Miss Wirble came back into the room.

"What on earth has been going on here?" she cried.

"Rufus rescued Mortimer and the fish," the class said.

"HMM," said Miss Wirble. "Maybe you're not such a wild animal, after all, Rufus."

Everyone cheered.